ATMOSPHERE

SEA OF AIR

EARTHWORKS

ATMOSPHERE

SEA OF AIR

ROY A. GALLANT

BENCHMARK BOOKS

MARSHALL CAVENDISH
NEW YORK

For Martha

Series Consultants:

LIFE SCIENCES AND ECOLOGY

Dr. Edward J. Kormondy
Chancellor and Professor of Biology (retired)
University of Hawaii—Hilo/West Oahu

PHYSICAL SCIENCES

Christopher J. Schuberth
Professor of Geology and Science Education
Armstrong Atlantic State University
Savannah, Georgia

Benchmark Books
Marshall Cavendish
99 White Plains Road
Tarrytown, NY 10591-9001

Library of Congress Cataloging-in-Publication Data
Gallant, Roy A.
Atmosphere:sea of air / by Roy A. Gallant
p. cm. — (EarthWorks series)
Includes bibliographical references and index.
Summary: Describes the atmosphere which makes life on Earth possible, explores its effects
on weather and climate, and examines what causes air pollution and what can be done
about it.
ISBN 0-7614-1366-9
1. Atmosphere—Juvenile literature. 2. Meterorology—Juvenile literature.
[1. Atmosphere. 2. Meterorology.] I. Title. II. Series.
QC863.5 .G35 2002
551.51-dc21   2001043301

Photo research by Linda Sykes Picture Research, Hilton Head, SC

Cover photo: Minden Pictures © Carr Clifton
The photographs in this book are used by permission and through the courtesy of:
Dani/Jeske/Earth Scenes: 1–2, 48–49; NASA: 6; John Meehan/Photo Researchers: 17;
Joel Sartore/National Geographic Image Sales: 29; E. R. Degginger/Earth Scenes, 32,
back cover; Tom Bean/Corbis: 34–35; Robert Fields/Earth Scenes: 37, back cover; Donald
Specker/Earth Scenes: 38, back cover; Arthur Glor/Earth Scenes: 40, back cover; Michael
Marten/Science Photo Library/Photo Researchers: 44; John Noble/Corbis: 47; Orbimage:
50–51; David Fritts/Earth Scenes: 52–53; Lineair/Peter Arnold: 55; Still Pictures/Peter
Arnold: 56; National Geographic: 57; Georg Gerster/Photo Researchers: 58–59,
back cover; Frans Lanting/Minden Pictures: 61; David Dennis/Earth Scenes: 63.

Series design by Edward Miller.

Printed in Hong Kong

1   3   5   6   4   2

CONTENTS

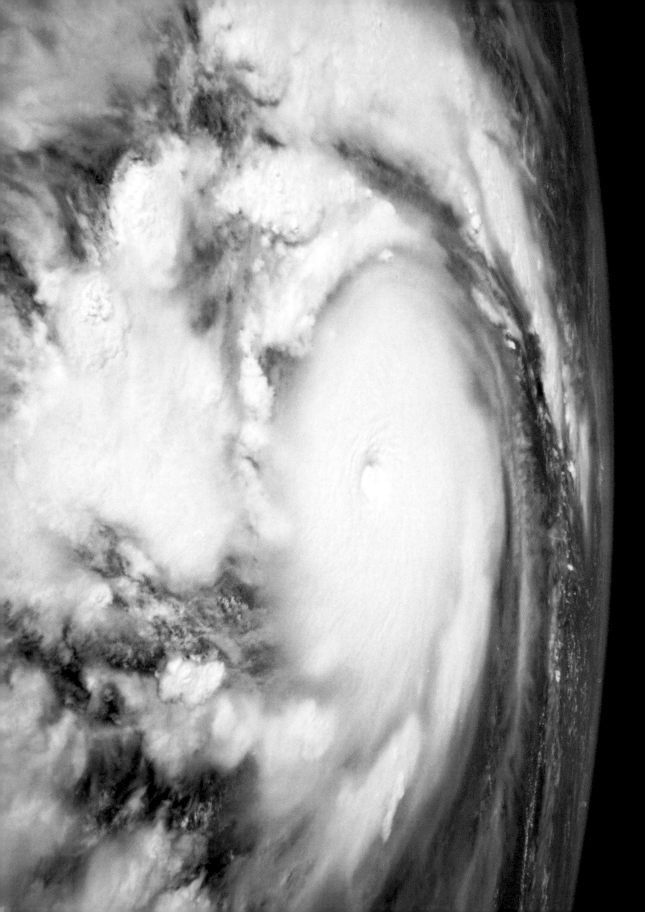

INTRODUCTION

We can imagine ourselves as living on the floor of an ocean of air. Held captive by Earth's gravity, this vast reservoir of air surrounds the planet for hundreds of miles. At the bottom we are safe and comfortable, and the air suits us perfectly. But if we were drawn up near the top, we would find it impossible to breathe and would die instantly.

Life on Earth depends on the air around us. Take our atmosphere away and there would be no trees, no animals, no clouds, and no colorful sunsets. Without the pressure of the air, all the oceans would boil away. The planet would be eerily quiet, for sound cannot travel through a vacuum. Earth would eventually be as dead and silent as the Moon. By day radiation from the Sun would travel unfiltered to Earth's surface, scorching everything in its path. By night temperatures would plunge to more than a hundred degrees below the freezing point, for there would be no atmosphere to trap and hold heat. As a greenhouse provides heat to its plants, our atmosphere works in much the same way, preventing Earth's stored heat from escaping into space.

The atmosphere is a mixture of many gases, dust, and more additional materials than you can imagine. A little more than three-quarters of the air is the gas nitrogen, an *element* that is important as a food for plants. Most of the remaining gas is oxygen, on which almost all of Earth's organisms depend. The rest of the atmosphere contains a number of different gases, some useful, some not. Two of the most important gases are carbon dioxide and water vapor. Both play central roles in helping to shape our planet's climate.

The atmosphere is the right mixture of gases that have sustained an enormous variety of life on Earth for hundreds of millions of years. With each breath, your lungs are enriched with oxygen, which your blood then carries to the billions of cells in your body. It is the breath of life. Without it, we would not survive.

A gigantic hurricane, as seen from space, swirls around in the central eye as it rages in Earth's lower atmosphere, where nearly all of our weather occurs. The punch that just one hurricane delivers can be greater than many atomic bombs and can pack enough energy to drive all the world's power stations for at least four years.

ONE

EARTH GETS AN ATMOSPHERE

Our Solar System is about 4.6 billion years old. At least that is the estimated age scientists have come up with when they use instruments such as radiation counters to measure the decay rates of certain radioactive substances in Earth's rocks. The oldest Earth rocks scientists have found so far are zircon crystals that are 4.03 billion years old. There must have been still older rocks that we can't date because they long ago melted and resolidified—over and over again. We don't know for sure because Earth's rocks are continually being recycled by this process. Meteorites that have crashed into Earth's surface are the oldest-known pieces of the Solar System. Some are as much as 4.6 billion years old.

But how did the Sun and its planets form? To try and find out, we turn our telescopes to certain regions of deep space where we can observe new stars being born. The birthplaces of stars are enormous clouds of gas and dust (silicate- and carbon-based minerals) that collapse in on themselves and become fiery suns. Like the other stars, our Sun was created from just such a giant cloud of mostly hydrogen gas and tiny clumps of material called space dust. As all that matter collapsed and packed itself into a ball, it grew extremely hot and began to spin, spreading into a great wheeling disk that stretched out for billions of miles. As it cooled, it clumped together into solid objects called *planetesimals*. Some were rock, others metal, and still others were ices of various substances, including water, ammonia, and methane.

FROM PLANETESIMALS TO PLANETS

Some planetesimals collided and shattered. But the larger ones did not break up. Instead their gravity swept up smaller ones, and so they grew into the huge spheres that today are the planets. For perhaps a hundred million years planetesimals rained down onto Earth. As they did, they heated our young planet to some 3600 degrees Fahrenheit (2000 °C) until it became a soupy ball of molten rock and metals. The metals sank into the planet's core, where they remain to this day as a great ball of iron and nickel. The lighter rocky materials, mostly *silicates*, floated to the surface and later cooled, becoming the planet's relatively thin crust. Eventually the rain of the planetesimals, along with the shower of countless comets, slowed to a drizzle.

During these early stages of Earth's history, gases bubbled out of the surface and began to collect above the new planet as a primitive atmosphere. They rose from the thousands of volcanoes that dotted Earth's landscape and boiled up through cracks in the ocean floor. From 80 to 85 percent of this outgassing, as the venting of gases is called, took place in about a million years. The rest of the gases were added over the next 4 billion years. They included large amounts of hydrogen, water vapor, carbon monoxide, and some methane and ammonia. The air was also thick with poisonous cyanide and formaldehyde and contained hydrochloric acid and sulfur dioxide. But most of the atmosphere was made up of nitrogen and carbon dioxide.

During those long centuries and millennia of outgassing, ultraviolet energy from the Sun broke down some of the complex gases in Earth's air. Ultraviolet energy is what gives us a sunburn. It changed ammonia into free hydrogen and nitrogen, methane into carbon and hydrogen, and water

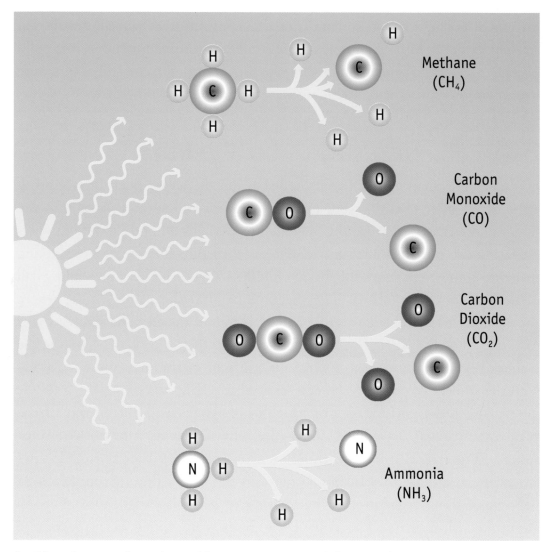

Earth's early atmosphere changed in many ways we can't be sure about. However, some things we do know: energy from the Sun broke down methane into free hydrogen and carbon atoms. Ammonia was broken down into free hydrogen and nitrogen.

vapor into hydrogen and oxygen. The free hydrogen was so light that most of it escaped Earth's gravity and floated off into space. The carbon dioxide in the air mixed with rainwater and made carbonic acid, the weak acid that is able to slowly erode stone and today melts the sharp features of marble and sandstone statues.

Perhaps some 400 million years after Earth formed a cool and stable rock crust, its atmosphere was mainly nitrogen, carbon dioxide, and water vapor, along with small amounts of the elements argon, neon, and other gases. Gone were the ammonia and methane of former times. Still to come was the age of oxygen, which possibly began some 2 billion years ago. We now think it was triggered by the appearance of certain oxygen-producing organisms called *cyanobacteria*. Broad and colorful blankets of cyanobacteria stretched from horizon to horizon during this time. They made their food by combining carbon dioxide and water vapor from the air in the presence of sunlight and giving off oxygen as a form of waste.

By around 600 million years ago, the slow buildup of oxygen had reached today's level of about 21 percent. The remaining 78 percent of the air is practically all nitrogen, with one percent made up mostly of argon with traces of carbon dioxide, ozone, methane, and many other gases.

Still, it would be wrong to think that Earth's air has remained the same since the oxygen revolution. Earth's history as a planet is marked by change, not by stability. The continents wander about, carried on the backs of *crustal plates*, those large rafts of solid rock that form Earth's crust. The oceans spread or shrink, and inland seas come and go. And so the percentages of different gases in the planet's air change as well. These shifts occur over long periods of time, but the planet's geological clock ticks so slowly that the changes are hardly noticeable.

DISCOVERING THE NATURE OF AIR

We have known what air is made of for a little more than 350 years. Until the 1600s many scientists still looked to the four "elements" ancient Greek thinkers had proposed some 2,000 years earlier. All matter, they claimed, was made of four root substances—earth, air, fire, and water. Trees, houses, clouds, and all other things were only a mingling of these four basic building blocks.

Not until the year 1661 did the English chemist Robert Boyle give the word element the meaning it has today. He said that four substances alone

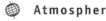 Atmosphere

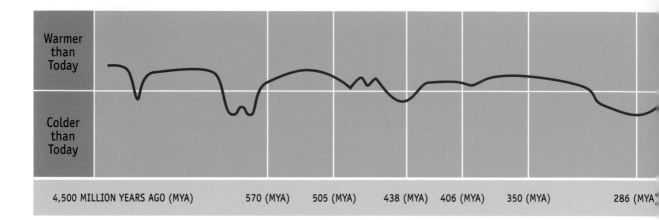

We know little about Earth's early temperature record, but we can estimate the temperatures beginning with the fossil record. As the climate changed, so did the life forms. For example, warm, swampy conditions were good for amphibians and some insects. Much later, mammoths, giant cats, and beavers thrived in the cold climate of the most recent ice age.

couldn't begin to account for all the chemical changes we observe in nature. So he set out to offer a new explanation. First he melted gold, then silver. Next, he mixed them with other metals and examined them again. No matter what he did to them, they did not change. They were true elements. Today an element is defined as a substance that can neither be broken down into nor built up from simpler substances by chemical means.

We now know of more than 110 different elements, of which some are solids and others gases. While nitrogen, oxygen, and argon are gaseous elements, there are also gaseous *compounds* made up of two or more of these elements. Carbon and oxygen combine to form the compound carbon dioxide (CO_2). Nitrogen and oxygen make nitrogen dioxide (NO_2), while hydrogen and oxygen join to create water vapor (H_2O). It took many years before all of the air's gases were identified. The discovery of oxygen is especially important because it plays so many roles in Earth's chemical processes. Almost all life on our planet depends on this essential element.

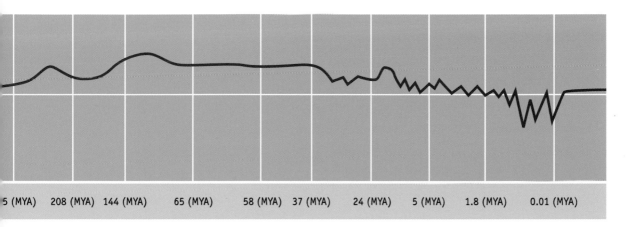

5 (MYA) 208 (MYA) 144 (MYA) 65 (MYA) 58 (MYA) 37 (MYA) 24 (MYA) 5 (MYA) 1.8 (MYA) 0.01 (MYA)

BECHER INVENTS PHLOGISTON

The story of oxygen begins with one of the most colorful men of science in the 1600s. Johann Joachim Becher was a German chemist who lived from 1635 to 1682. His wild ideas caused him to be chased out of nearly every major country in Europe. One of his schemes was to use silver and beach sand to make gold. Holy Roman Emperor Leopold I and his advisors were so convinced that Becher would succeed that they decided to build him a gold factory in Vienna and promised him all the money he would need to operate it—until they discovered that the plan wouldn't work.

Becher is perhaps best remembered for his part in developing the phlogiston theory to explain what occurred during combustion, or burning. His idea was simple and gained wide acceptance because it seemed to address a lot of questions about burning that at the time couldn't be answered any other way. Becher said that anything that could be set on fire contained a "fatty earth" substance, which he called *phlogiston* (from the Greek *phlogizein*, meaning "to set on fire"). It was this substance, Becher said, that became flame during burning.

He cited proof of his theory by claiming that phlogiston had weight, color, and an odor. To prove it has weight, he said, just burn something. Wood is reduced to ashes after it has been burned. And if you weigh the

13

ashes, you will find that they weigh less than the original wood. He said that the reason for this was that the phlogiston escaped from the wood as it was burning. The same is true of any object having phlogiston, he told his fellow chemists.

But was it true of any object? What about lead, some of Becher's critics asked? When lead is burned, the ashes that remain are *heavier* than the original piece of metal. How could he explain that, they asked? Becher had a ready answer. Phlogiston also has the property of levity, he explained. It sometimes weighs less than nothing. So when you remove it from certain substances, they will naturally weigh more than they did before they were burned. At the time no one could offer a better explanation of burning.

So Becher's theory gained acceptance. The science of chemistry was still in its youth, and the only thing chemists of the time were sure of was that when a piece of wood, for instance, burned, particles of some kind were released. Today we know that those particles are the parts of atoms called *electrons* and that the cause of burning is oxygen from the air combining with the substance being burned, in a process called *rapid oxidation*. But in the seventeenth-century, scientists had a limited understanding of the atom, so Becher's phlogiston particles seemed a reasonable explanation.

Priestley Makes Oxygen

The story next moves to the year 1774 and the laboratory of Joseph Priestley, an Englishman for whom chemistry was a hobby. A century earlier, Robert Boyle had shown that some part of the air supported not only burning, but life as well. He discovered this by placing a burning candle and a mouse under a large bell jar and observing what happened. Eventually, the candle flame grew weak and finally went out. As it did, the mouse also grew weak and died.

Priestley was fascinated by this mysterious part of the air and determined to find out what it was. Today, of course, we know that it was oxygen. Priestley first made oxygen by focusing the Sun's rays through a large magnifying lens onto a tube containing mercuric oxide, a compound of mercury and oxygen. As the mercury heated, it broke down and released oxygen as a gas. Priestley was then able to collect the oxygen in a tube. When he held a lit candle in the tube, the flame burned brightly. A glowing piece of charcoal burst into flame. And a mouse placed under a bell jar filled with oxygen lived longer than another mouse placed under a bell jar filled with ordinary air.

What should he call this gas that was necessary to both fire and life? Since flames died out when the gas was used up, he decided to call it dephlogisticated air, that is, air with its phlogiston removed. Although Priestley's work disproved the phlogiston theory, he remained a firm believer in phlogiston his entire life. The French chemist Antoine Lavoisier, who lived from 1743 to 1794, recognized "dephlogisticated" air as a true element and named it *oxygen*.

Boyle's "Spring of Air"

Robert Boyle had also discovered that air could be compressed or squeezed into a smaller space. It is just such compression of the atmosphere that makes the air pressure near the ground greater than the air pressure at higher altitudes. Boyle called this mysterious property "the spring of air." From his experiments he concluded that if you squeeze any amount of air into one half its space, you will double its pressure.

Scientists were inching closer to a more complete understanding of Earth's atmosphere and the ways in which its gases behave. It was Boyle's work with the spring of air that provided the first ideas about *atmospheric pressure*. We can picture the atmosphere as a tall stack of feather pillows. The weight of the pillows higher up tends to compress those pillows farther down. That is why there is greater air pressure at ground level than higher up. Boyle would have been fascinated to know that he helped shape our understanding of the atmosphere—from its many layers to its always shifting, always fascinating weather patterns.

TWO

OUR
OCEAN OF AIR

If we could gather all of Earth's air into a big box, it would weigh about 6,000 trillion tons. That's equal to the weight of more than 33 billion large railway engines. It's hard to believe that air can weigh that much. In addition to the gases that occur naturally in the atmosphere, the air contains a host of other ingredients—particles spewed from volcanoes, salt grains from sea spray, dust released by meteors streaking across the sky, sand blown by desert storms, soot from forest fires, rubber vaporized from car tires, pollen grains from plants, bacteria, and the spores of fungi. In addition, there are many chemicals floating in the air in the form of fertilizers and pesticides, dust, and other human wastes. Fortunately, there is so much atmosphere that it can hold the millions of tons of particles and polluting gases that we pour into the air day and night. Unfortunately, pollution poses a great risk to the plants, and animals, including people, who have to breathe that air.

Even nature causes pollution by pouring greenhouse gases, ash, and other aerosols into the global circulation. This occurs during volcanic episodes, such as the 1980 eruption of Mount St. Helens.

THE SKY IS THE LIMIT

The atmosphere is made up of layers that lack sharp boundaries. Each layer has its own range of pressure and temperature that makes it distinct from the layer above or below. Let's start with the layer that is closest to the ground and then work our way up.

Troposphere   This lowest layer contains 99 percent of all our planet's air. It is the most crowded with gas molecules, smoke, and countless other particles. At sea level more than a ton of air presses against you from all sides. Here the atmospheric pressure is 14.7 pounds per square inch (6.7 kilograms per square centimeter), and a gas molecule can travel only a few millionths of an inch before bumping into another one. Almost all of our weather occurs within the troposphere. At the latitude of the United States, the layer reaches up to about 41,000 feet (12,500 meters), or nearly 8 miles (13 kilometers). On a hot August day, the air temperature at the bottom of the troposphere may be 95 degrees Fahrenheit (35 °C), but at the top it averages –70 degrees Fahrenheit (–57 °C). Temperature in this layer drops at an average rate of about 3.5 degrees Fahrenheit per 1,000 feet (6 °C per 305 meters). The reason for this temperature gradient, or change with altitude, is that heat radiated from Earth's surface warms the air closest to the ground more than it warms the air higher up.

Air in the troposphere moves over the land as wind. As the Sun heats large, flat areas of land, the air near the ground becomes lighter and rises, creating vertical air currents. While the lower *troposphere* contains large amounts of water vapor, the top layer holds relatively little.

Stratosphere   This second layer of the atmosphere begins wherever the troposphere ends and goes up to a height of about 30 miles (50 kilometers). Like the upper troposphere, the lower regions of the *stratosphere* are extremely cold and are swept by strong winds. Higher up, however, the winds taper off and the temperature gradually rises, except over the polar regions in winter. But then, at the top of the stratosphere, a strong river of wind called the *jet stream* attains high speeds of some 300 miles (480 kilometers) per hour. Up here the temperature is about 30 degrees Fahrenheit (–1 °C).

The cause of this sudden warming is a layer of the gas ozone. Ozone is a form of oxygen that has three atoms (O_3) instead of two (O_2), which is the type of oxygen we breathe. A blanket of ozone in the upper stratosphere blocks out most of the high-energy ultraviolet radiation from the Sun. Without the protective layer, living organisms exposed to the full force of *ultraviolet radiation* would be seriously harmed. Atmospheric pressure at the top of the stratosphere is only 1/1,000 of the pressure at sea level, which makes it about the same as being in deep space.

Mesosphere   Resting on top of the stratosphere is that feather-pillow layer called the *mesosphere*. It is about 20 miles (30 kilometers) deep. Here temperatures are even lower, 30 degrees Fahrenheit (–1 °C) at the base, and then bottoming out at about –130 degrees Fahrhenheit (–90 °C) near the top. At this height the air is so diffuse, or thin, that hardly any light is scattered about by the decreased numbers of gas *molecules*. The result is that the sky no longer appears blue, but is nearly black. At an altitude of some 60 miles (97 kilometers) a gas molecule can travel about 1 inch (2.5 centimeters) before colliding with another one. The air becomes so diffuse in the mesosphere that sound can no longer travel through it.

Thermosphere   Topping the mesosphere is the fourth major layer of air— the *thermosphere*. It is the borderline of space. At the lowest part of the thermosphere the temperature begins to rise again. It increases from –130 degrees Fahrenheit (–90 °C) at the base to more than 2000 degrees Fahrenheit (1093 °C) at the "top." But it is impossible to say at what height the top of the atmosphere "ends." The uppermost part of the atmosphere is somewhere between 260 and 900 miles (418 and 1,450 kilometers) above

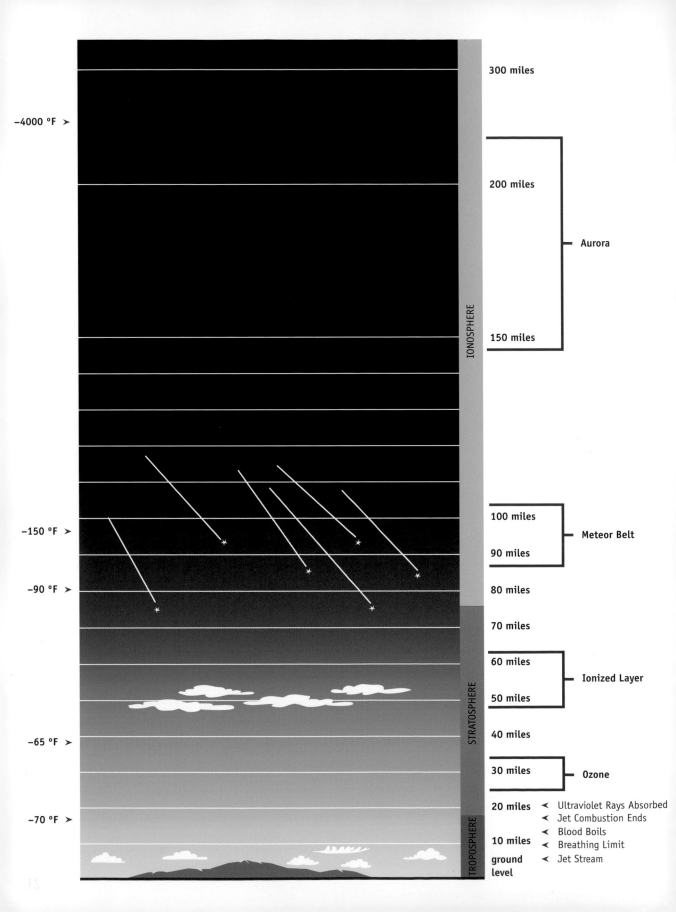

300 miles

−4000 °F ➤

200 miles

Aurora

150 miles

IONOSPHERE

100 miles

Meteor Belt

−150 °F ➤

90 miles

80 miles

−90 °F ➤

70 miles

60 miles

Ionized Layer

50 miles

STRATOSPHERE

40 miles

−65 °F ➤

30 miles   Ozone

20 miles ◄ Ultraviolet Rays Absorbed
          ◄ Jet Combustion Ends
          ◄ Blood Boils
−70 °F ➤   ◄ Breathing Limit
10 miles ◄ Jet Stream

TROPOSPHERE

ground
level

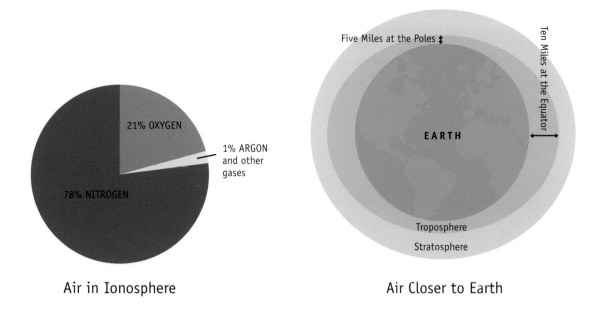

Air in Ionosphere

Air Closer to Earth

We live at the bottom of a deep ocean of air. At ground level, the air is a dense mixture of gases. The higher we go, the "thinner" the air becomes. The last traces of atmosphere are hundreds or thousands of miles above the planet.

The lowest air layer, the troposphere, is where Earth has weather. Above, at the top of the stratosphere, the sky darkens significantly. The top of the ionosphere is the border with space. Cosmic rays, dangerous ultraviolet rays, and most meteoroids are blocked from reaching us in dangerous concentrations at ground level. Without the atmosphere, all land and sea life would perish. Only bacteria that live underground would survive.

Earth. Here a gas molecule can travel 2,000 miles (3,220 kilometers) before bumping into its neighbor.

Since there are so few molecules in the thermosphere, there is no transfer of heat. The high temperatures up here are simply a measure of the speed of gas molecules. Any living creature taken up into the thermosphere and exposed to its thin air would be broiled to death on the side facing the Sun and frozen to death on the side in shadow. And due to the virtual lack of atmospheric pressure, the body's fluids would instantly boil in a condition called *explosive decompression*. Back down in the troposphere, the atmospheric pressure is high enough to prevent this from happening.

THE ATMOSPHERE IN MOTION

The air surrounding our planet is continually moving. And for the most part we can count on it to move in certain predictable ways. While there are local motions of air, such as winds and vertical currents, there are also large wind systems that move in fairly regular patterns around Earth. These are due to a combination of Earth spinning around on its axis and the Sun heating the air.

The major wind systems that circulate most of the air around the globe occur in seven belts. We count the Equator as one belt. There are three more belts in the Northern Hemisphere and three in the Southern Hemisphere: *trade winds*, *prevailing westerlies*, and *polar easterlies*.

Throughout the year, the Sun's energy falls most intensely on a broad belt extending just north and south of the Equator. All along the sunlit section of this belt, over land and sea alike, Earth's surface and the air above are heated. This heating creates a *low-pressure system* of rising air. Low-pressure air is simply air with its gas molecules spaced relatively far apart. So a portion of it is lighter than an equal amount of high-pressure air, whose gas molecules are packed more tightly together, making it heavier. It is like the air above a radiator—it becomes heated, expands, and rises because it is lighter than the cold air around it.

As the Equator's low-pressure air rises high above the ground, it is cooled, becomes heavy, and tends to sink back down again. But a steady flow of hot, rising air pushing up from below prevents it from doing so. This much warmer air is filled with moisture in the form of water vapor. As it is cooled at a higher altitude, the water vapor condenses into clouds and then into rain, providing the land areas of the Equatorial belt with abundant rainfall.

The belt of air girdling the Equator is carried along at the rotational speed of Earth's surface at the Equator—about 1,000 miles (1,600 kilometers) per hour. Because the Equatorial air and the ground below it are moving at the same speed, about the only motion the Equatorial air has is upward. So the little wind that blows is usually light and variable, and those parts of the belt of air that lie over the oceans are often calm. In the past, sailors of the old ships driven by wind and sail dreaded this part of the ocean, where for days on end their ships drifted slowly under the blistering tropical Sun. They called this belt of calm the *doldrums*.

As the Equatorial air rises, some of it streams north toward the North Pole while some of it branches off in the opposite direction in the south. At about 30 degrees north and south latitudes, some of the air dips down toward Earth's surface. Here it tends to pile up and form the *high-pressure system* called the *horse latitudes*. In general, the air here is fairly calm, or if there are winds, they are light and variable. The climate of the horse latitudes is generally sunny, hot, and dry. Some of the world's great desert regions—northern Mexico, northern Africa, and northern India—lie along this belt.

The high-pressure air at the horse latitudes doubles back and flows close to Earth's surface toward the Equator, replacing the rising Equatorial air. It forms a broad belt called the *trade winds*, which blow rather steadily. Because of Earth's rotational speed at this latitude, which is slower than at the Equator, the trade winds travel at a slant instead of looping straight southward back to the Equator. In the Northern Hemisphere they move from northeast to southwest and are called the *northeast trades*. In the Southern Hemisphere they blow from the southeast to the northwest and are called the *southeast trades*.

From about 35 degrees north and south latitudes to about 55 degrees is another wind belt, the prevailing westerlies. In the Northern Hemisphere they blow from the southwest to the northeast. In the Southern Hemisphere they flow from the northwest to the southeast. This wind belt has its source in the stream of air flowing north and south from the Equator. In the latitudes of the westerlies the air moves faster than Earth's rotational speed. So, like the trade winds, the westerlies travel at a slant, but in the opposite direction.

Similarly, the westerlies also blow steadily day and night at Earth's surface. But their effect is greatest at altitudes where airplanes fly. A jet traveling east

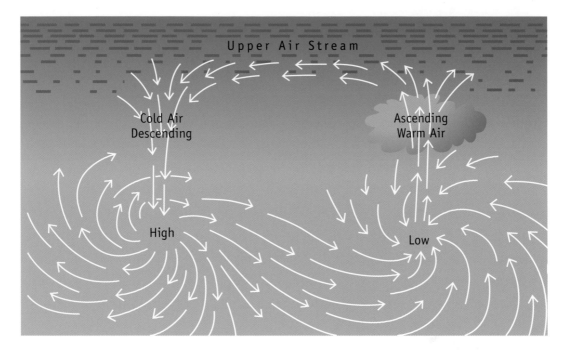

At left, cool air flowing down from the upper air stream piles up and forms a high-pressure system. At right, warm air that rises into the air stream above leaves a low-pressure system. Winds always blow from a region of high pressure to a region of low pressure.

from New York to London is carried along by the westerlies and can make the trip in about two hours less time than it takes for the return flight back to New York.

Mountains, valleys, plains, and other features of Earth's surface interfere with the flow of the westerlies at ground level. This is one reason that we do not feel the steady force of the westerlies at the surface. Warm moist air moving up from the south and cold dry air moving down from the north cross paths with the westerlies. This adds to the ever-changing winds and variety of storms that make the westerlies our most active weather belt. Whenever the course of the westerlies over certain regions of Earth alters temporarily, those areas experience marked changes in weather and in *climate*. For example, researchers now think that certain Indian cultures that vanished about a thousand years ago in the American Southwest were driven off their land by long periods of drought.

Some of the warm moist air that leaves the Equator makes it all the way to the polar ice caps. But by the time it arrives at the top and bottom of the world, it has been cooled and nearly all of its moisture has been wrung out. This air tends to pile up over the poles, where it forms a high-pressure cap. Because the air moves more slowly than Earth's rotational speed at these high latitudes, the winds called the polar easterlies blow in the same south-slanting direction as the trade winds.

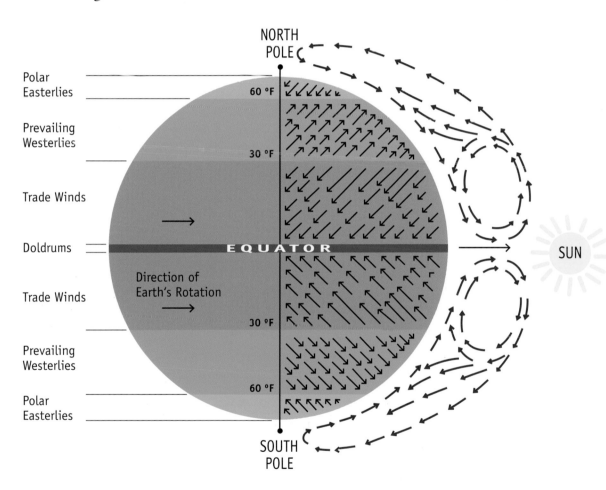

Earth's global air circulation is set in motion by heat from the Sun. As air above the Equator becomes heated, it rises and flows off toward the poles. Because the planet's speed of rotation at ground level changes with latitude, something called the Coriolis effect causes the trade winds to blow in a direction opposite that of the westerlies.

THE JET STREAM

The jet stream snakes its way around the globe near the bottom of the stratosphere at an altitude of some 30,000 feet (9,000 meters). This blustery current frequently blows at 300 miles (480 kilometers) per hour.

The winter jet stream blows strongest and may dip south to just below Florida. It is strongest as it leaves the coast of Asia and travels across Africa toward India. The summer jet stream slows a bit and moves farther north toward the Arctic Circle. At times it sweeps down toward the Equator but then wends its way back toward the Arctic. Up to 100 miles (160 kilometers) wide and 1 mile (1.6 kilometers) deep, the jet stream tends to flow along the border of the polar easterlies and the prevailing westerlies.

When the jet stream loops southward, it brings cold polar air with it and may cause unusually chilly springtime weather in Florida. At the same time another loop may draw warmer air north and cause an autumn heat wave in Maine. There also is a jet stream in the Southern Hemisphere. Airline pilots usually avoid hitching a ride in the jet stream, even though its strong winds can cause a plane to zip along at great speeds. The reason is that the jet stream air is very rough and can bounce a plane around and violently shake its passengers.

The major wind systems that girdle Earth determine how the atmosphere circulates. But they don't always follow a predictable and precise path. As described here they are "ideal" systems. We have not considered the effect of mountains, valleys, and other land features. And there are the changing seasons, the ocean currents, and other things that have to be taken into account. These various factors can cause the slightest change or a major disturbance, such as thunderstorms, hurricanes, and tornadoes that can whip up with only a brief warning and cause serious harm. Let's find out how nature brews such violent concoctions.

THREE

VIOLENT STORMS

A hurricane is the most destructive kind of storm. The forces driving a hurricane are raging winds, lashing rains, and angry seas. In 1992, Hurricane Andrew caused twenty-six deaths and $30 billion in damages. A hurricane in Bangladesh a year earlier killed more than 125,000 people and caused about $2 billion in damages. Whenever Earth's atmosphere goes on a rampage, we realize just how powerless we are when compared with the forces of nature.

HURRICANES

Hurricanes are known by several names. Pacific Islanders call them typhoons. The Australians refer to them as willy-willies, and around the Indian Ocean they are known as cyclones.

Hurricanes begin over the ocean near the Equator, in the doldrums. For days and weeks the blistering Sun beats down on the calm ocean water. Slowly the air above the sea becomes heated and begins to spiral lazily overhead. More hot moist air is sucked in and drawn skyward. Gradually this circle of twisting air grows, spinning faster and faster counterclockwise. As

Destruction from hurricanes is often devastating. This trailer park in Homestead, Florida, was flattened by Hurricane Andrew in 1992, and hundreds were left homeless.

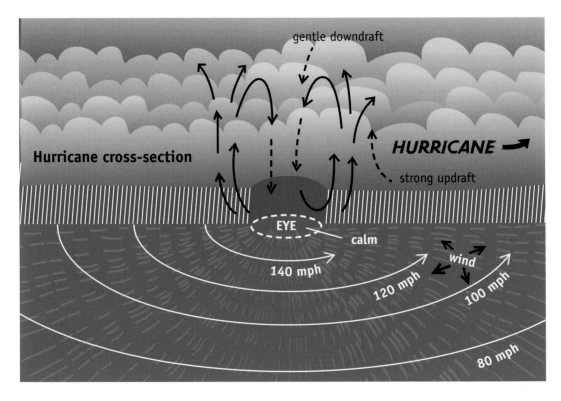

During a hurricane, the wind circles counterclockwise around the central eye, which ranges from 15 to 60 miles (24 to 100 kilometers) in width.

the air around the top of the spiral cools, rain clouds form. With a near limitless fuel supply of hot moist air below the circling winds, the storm system grows.

Inside the spiral is a circle of calm known as the hurricane's eye. Directly overhead there is often clear blue sky, but around the rim rage rain and winds of 150 to 200 miles (240 to 320 kilometers) per hour. The eye of a hurricane ranges from 15 to 60 miles (24 to 100 kilometers) across. The clouds marking the width of the storm may span an area of some 600 miles (965 kilometers) or more. If you have ever been through a hurricane, you know about their fierce rains. In the early 1900s, a severe hurricane that struck Luzon in the Philippines dropped nearly 4 feet (122 centimeters) of water in 24 hours.

Hurricane season is between August and October. Once a hurricane is on the warpath and heads toward land, it sends out several warnings. One is unusually high tides. Others are an advancing low-pressure area and high feathery clouds that cause a ring around the Moon. Later, towering thunder-clouds boil up and darken the sky. The rains and wind then ravage the land.

TORNADOES

Closely related to the hurricane, a tornado is a black weaving vacuum funnel that can suck animals, automobiles, and even entire houses into its hungry mouth. Like most violent storms, a tornado is caused by a clash between warm moist air and cold dry air. Three-quarters of the world's tornadoes occur in the Midwestern United States in what is known as Tornado Alley—an area stretching from Texas through Oklahoma, Missouri, Kansas, Nebraska, and South Dakota.

On hot summer days people who live in the tornado belt grow anxious when the skies darken and they sense a thunderstorm is on the way. Warm air rich in water vapor flows from the Gulf of Mexico and the Caribbean Sea. At the same time, cold dry air passing over the Rocky Mountains and carried by the prevailing westerlies settles on top of the warm air. Where the two layers touch, rain clouds begin to brew and a storm is born. The warm air below starts to spin around a hollow center. As the spiral whips around faster and faster, it creates a tornado, a deadly funnel that zigzags across the land.

Winds sweeping around the funnel reach speeds of 300 miles (480 kilometers) an hour. Like a giant vacuum cleaner, the funnel wanders overland at 25 to 40 miles (40 to 64 kilometers) per hour, drawing in nearly every-thing in its path. When it passes over a building, the building usually explodes. Tightly packed high-pressure air inside the building expands so rapidly that it pushes the walls out in all directions and blows the roof off into the low-pressure air of the tornado. Some of the leftover debris is then sucked up into the tornado's funnel and carried away.

A tornado often zigzags its way along unpredictably, its fierce snout sucking up all in its path—tractors, kitchen stoves, and even cows. The extreme low-pressure air around the funnel of a tornado causes the high-pressure air to blow out the walls of any building in its path.

Unlike hurricanes, tornadoes sweep over a narrow tract of land. They are seldom more than 1,000 feet (300 meters) across, and these storms usually peter out after traveling a few miles. One of the things that makes them terrifying, though, is that you can never be sure where they are going. For a while one may boom along in a straight path, then suddenly shift to the left, then weave back to the right. People watching a tornado can only hope that the funnel will not sweep over them. When a tornado occurs over the ocean, it sucks up huge amounts of water and is known as a waterspout.

One of the most vivid descriptions of a tornado ever written appeared in the May 1930 issue of *Monthly Weather Review*. It was written by Will Keller, a Greenburg, Kansas, farmer who lived through one of these ferocious storms.

> At last the great shaggy end of the funnel hung directly overhead. Everything was as still as death. There was a strong gassy odor, and it seemed as though I could not breathe. There was a screaming, hissing sound coming directly from the end of the funnel. I looked up, and to my astonishment saw right into the heart of the tornado. There was a circular opening in the center of the funnel about 15 to 30 meters [50 to 100 feet] in diameter, and extending straight upward for a distance of at least half a mile. The walls were rotating clouds and the hole was brilliantly lighted with constant flashes of lightning which zigzagged from side to side.

> After it passed my place it again dipped and struck and demolished the house and barn of a farmer by the name of Evans. . . . Not having time to reach their cellar, they took refuge under a small bluff that faced to the leeward of the approaching tornado. They lay down flat on the ground and caught hold of some plum bushes which fortunately grew within their reach. As it was, they felt themselves lifted from the ground. Mr. Evans said that he could see the wreckage of his house, among it being the cook stove going round and round over his head.

THUNDERSTORMS

At least once during the summer you can count on being caught in a thunderstorm. The most common sign that a storm is coming is the appearance of a majestic thunderhead cloud, the cumulonimbus. The afternoon may be clear and hot with the Sun beating down on a nearby field. But a storm is in the making. The heat from the field causes the moist hot air over it to rise. Once it is high enough, water vapor in the air cools and condenses, and a cloud is formed. If these moist air currents are strong enough, they continue to push even higher into the troposphere, where the water vapor turns into ice crystals. As the cloud builds, water vapor condenses into rain, and the storm begins, signaled by flashing lightning and booming thunder. At the top of the cloud there may be hail, snow, and sleet, but it seldom reaches the ground. Warmer parts of the cloud and hot air below melt the ice and snow as they fall.

When a thundercloud unleashes its torrents of rain, the drops clean the air by sweeping out fine ash, salt, dust, and many chemicals. Among the chemicals are traces of sulfur and nitrogen, both of which enrich the soil with nutrients and help make it more fertile.

Strong updrafts and downdrafts within the cloud can turn it into a hail factory. Small pellets of ice

Thunder and lightning storms are not just dramatic events that disrupt our day. The huge amounts of rain released by thunderclouds actually clean the air we breathe.

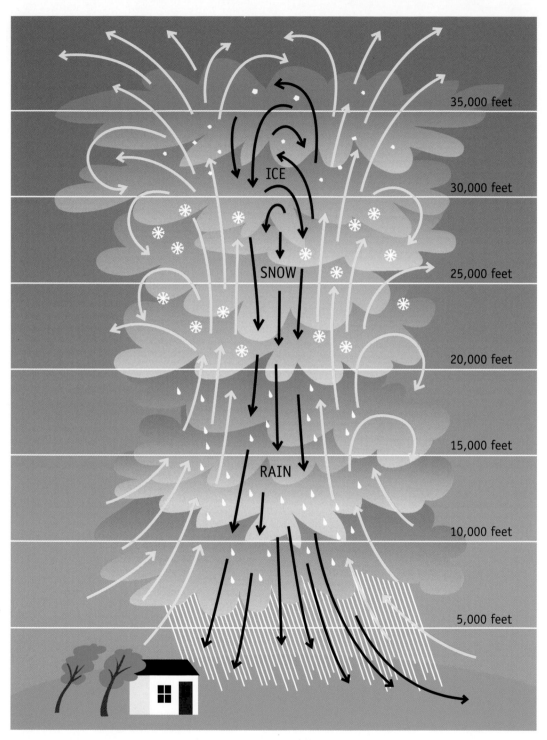

Updrafts and downdrafts within a thundercloud are violent. While relatively high tempera-tures may be at the base of the cloud, severe cold at the top produces snow and ice that eventually may grow heavy enough to fall out of the cloud as hail.

36

One sign of a fully developed thunderhead is the anvil shape at the top, stretched out by strong winds. Updrafts and downdrafts within the cloud are fierce.

formed in the upper regions of the cloud fall but are caught by an updraft and lifted again to the top of the cloud. The film of water collected by a pellet on its way up is frozen, and so it grows heavier and plummets again. But it still doesn't reach the ground. Once more it collects another coating of water and is carried back up, where that too freezes. Repeated trips up and down within the cloud can create a hailstone the size of a lemon or larger. Finally, when the ball of ice is heavy enough, it tumbles to the ground and can turn your sundeck into a skating rink.

If you were to cut a hailstone in half to see how it is made, you would notice that it is composed of several layers, like an onion. Counting the layers would show how many trips the hailstone made to the top of the cloud before finally falling out. How large can a hailstone get? The heaviest on record was 2.3 pounds (1 kilogram) and fell in Bangladesh on April 14, 1986. Another hailstone that fell in Kansas in 1970 weighed 1.7 pounds (785 grams) and was 17.5 inches (about 45 centimeters) around.

Storms can be a stirring sight to witness, but the violent conditions that often occur within a thundercloud can also have tragic results. In 1930, during a flying contest in Germany's Rhöne Mountain region, five glider pilots got too close to a fierce thundercloud and found themselves helplessly drawn into

A storm of hailstones the size of marbles devastated this cornfield in Mohawk, New York, in a few minutes. Hailstones, which form near the tops of thunderhead clouds, may grow as big as tennis balls.

it. The strong winds within the cloud shredded their fragile craft. Trying to save themselves, they made the mistake of opening their parachutes while still in the cloud. Instead of falling out safely, they found that the billowing parachutes caught strong updrafts and catapulted them higher into the cloud's freezing upper regions. Huge raindrops pelted and soaked them while hailstones lashed their faces and bodies. We can only imagine what happened during those few desperate minutes. By the time they were carried to a height of some 50,000 feet (15,240 meters), they must have been encased in ice and tossed about on the surging winds until finally the cloud released them. Only one was lucky enough to parachute out of the cloud and survive.

Thunderstorms come complete with lightning and thunder. Strong updrafts, downdrafts, and crosscurrents within a cloud cause the cloud's particles to rub against each other so vigorously that electric charges are built up. You can make your own electric charge by scuffing your feet across a rug. If you then touch your finger to a brass doorknob or a friend's arm, you'll get a weak shock and see a little spark. This is what happens when lightning strikes, except that lightning packs more of a punch. If a negatively charged cloud passes over positively charged ground, the cloud releases a bolt of electrons in the form of lightning. Lightning can also strike from ground to cloud, from cloud to cloud, and within the same cloud.

The thunderclap you hear after a lightning flash is made by rapidly heated air that expands explosively along the surging path of electrons. The distant rumbling is caused by the thunder's sound waves bouncing back and forth within clouds or between nearby mountains.

The most spectacular action, in the form of a dazzling light show, takes place high above the thunderclouds at altitudes up to about 55 miles (90 kilometers). Avalanches of electrons charge the air and create towers and jets of blue light that stab into the stratosphere. Higher up, enormous red blobs with long tentacles dance and flicker, while higher still is a mysterious green glow.

To most of us, a lightning storm, with its booming thunder and fireworks, is hardly a frequent occurrence. But to people living in Bogor, Java, thunderstorms are routine. They light the sky an average of 322 days of the year.

FOUR

THE SKY AS A SOURCE OF WONDER

Point at a rainbow and you'll lose your finger, according to an ancient superstition. Earth's atmosphere is a fun house of spectacular light shows that seemed magical or terrifying to people in the past. Even today, some people are still perplexed and frightened when they first see the northern lights. Most of us, however, rarely even bother to examine the daytime or nighttime sky. Sadly, we miss many of our atmosphere's most dazzling and beautiful displays.

A double rainbow occurs when a second rainbow forms above the primary rainbow. What do you notice about the arrangement of colors in the two rainbows?

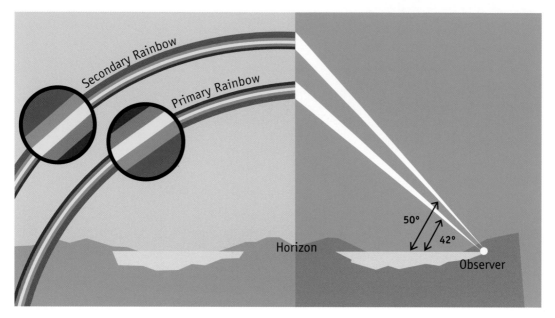

Faint or bright, the colors in a primary and secondary rainbow forming a double bow are always in the same order, but the color arrangement in the secondary rainbow is reversed compared to that in the primary rainbow.

On entering a raindrop, light gets refracted, or bent, then reflected, or bounced, off the back of the raindrop, and then refracted again on exiting the drop.

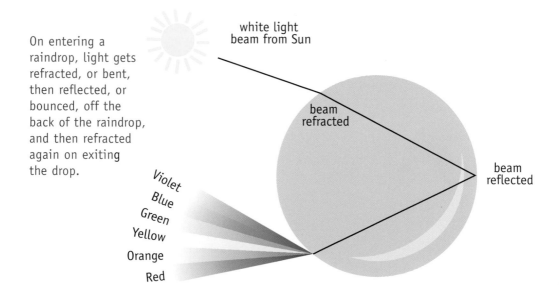

CHASING RAINBOWS

Usually we see rainbows after a rain shower or in the fine spray of a fountain, a waterfall, or a garden hose. The rainbow's bands of color appear in a half circle. From top to bottom, the order of the colors is always red, orange, yellow, green, blue, and violet. This array of hues is called the *primary rainbow*. Sometimes you can see a double rainbow, with a second arc curving above the primary one. If you look carefully, you will find that the order of colors in the secondary rainbow is backwards. You'll also notice that a darker band of sky divides the two rainbows. A morning rainbow is always found in the west, with the Sun behind you. Afternoon rainbows are always in the east, again with the Sun at your back.

To make a rainbow with a garden hose, just turn your back to the Sun and start spraying. The higher up you are, atop a small mountain, for instance, the more of the rainbow you will see. That's because a rainbow is actually a complete circle, but the bottom part of it is usually cut off by the horizon. So the higher you are, the more of the circle you will see. If you go still higher, as in an airplane, you may see a rainbow's full circle. That disproves another old superstition: there can't be a pot of gold at the end of a rainbow, because a rainbow doesn't have an end.

We see a rainbow when the Sun's light is refracted, or bent, as it enters tiny rain droplets in the air. Just as a glass prism refracts and separates white light into its individual colors, each tiny rain droplet does the same thing. When a beam of sunlight enters a raindrop, the white light is separated into its rainbow of colors. As the light beam is then reflected back out of the waterdrop, it is bent a second time and fans out even more, into a primary rainbow. Because there are billions of water droplets spread all over the sky, we see one large rainbow.

MAKING A RAINBOW

Any rounded glass makes a good experimental raindrop. Fill the glass with water, but not too full. In a darkened room, place a flashlight flat on some object at about shoulder height. Standing with your back to the flashlight beam but not blocking it, hold the glass by the bottom out in front of you at arm's length. Then move the glass to the left about a foot until you see some colors form. You may see a splash of color at first, but the color you are looking for is a bright red line near the side of the glass. It is a reflection off the opposite side of your "raindrop" glass.

When it enters the water, the flashlight beam is refracted, and it is refracted again when it leaves the glass. With the glass held straight out in front of you, all colors except red are bent so much they cannot be seen. Red remains visible because it is refracted least.

If you move the glass slightly in one direction, the red line disappears. Move it slightly in the opposite direction, and a color other than red appears. To see even more colors, arrange a half circle of small water-filled glasses around you. Since you will be viewing each glass from a different angle, you will see a different color in each one. The colors will range from blue at one end to red at the other end of your half circle—a complete water-glass rainbow.

Sun halos and Moon halos are caused by high cirrus clouds of ice crystals that reflect and refract light from the Moon or Sun. The inner edge of these halos is red, but the color brightness depends on the nature of the ice crystals.

WHY IS THE SKY BLUE?

Earth is called the "blue planet." Whether we look at it from a mountaintop, an ocean liner, or an airplane, the sky appears blue when there are no clouds. Some people think the ocean is blue and makes the sky the same color. But if you scoop up a bucket of ocean water and slowly pour it out, you will see it is no bluer than water from your kitchen tap. And since the Sun isn't blue, the color of the sky must have something to do with the atmosphere. But what?

As sunlight shines down through the air, it moves among the gas molecules and fine dust particles. Its rays then get bounced like a ball in a pinball machine, this way and that, and so they become scattered through the atmosphere. Because the white light of the Sun is actually made up of the individual colors we see in a rainbow, each of those colors travels through the air as waves. Red rays have the longest wavelengths, or distance from one wave crest to the next. Orange rays are not quite as long. The rays of the remaining colors decrease in wavelength, blue and violet being the shortest.

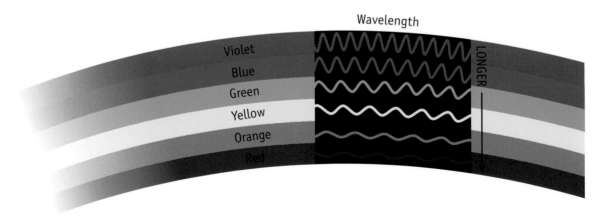

White light from the Sun is composed of a rainbow of colors made visible when the light is refracted through a prism, or in the atmosphere. Each color has its characteristic wavelength, violet and blue having the shortest wavelengths and red the longest. The blue wavelengths get scattered most by the atmosphere, which makes the sky look blue.

Because the shorter wavelengths of blue and violet are closer to the size of the gas molecules making up the air, those colors get scattered the most. They reach our eyes as the color blue. The higher we climb into the atmosphere the darker blue the sky becomes. The darkening occurs as the air thins and there are fewer and fewer gas molecules to scatter light. At the top of the atmosphere, and beyond, there are so few gas molecules that there is no scattering at all, just the blackness of space.

The next time you are driving near mountains on a clear day, notice how blue the distant peaks appear. The farther away you are from a distant object, the more air there is between you and the object to scatter blue light, so more blue light reaches your eyes. That is one reason why the ocean closer to the horizon—like those distant mountains—appears so blue.

Logically, we know that mountains are not actually blue, but when we see them from a great distance, they look that way because blue light gets scattered most by our atmosphere.

Another reason is that the tiny molecules of water scatter blue light very well, just as the tiny gas molecules of the air do. The deeper the sunlight shines down into the ocean, the bluer the water appears.

Since blue and violet wavelengths get scattered most, why do we have all those beautiful red and orange sunrises and sunsets? During the early morning and early evening hours, the Sun's rays must pass through the thickest part of the atmosphere. As they do, the shorter wavelengths—violet, blue, and green—are absorbed. Only the longest wavelengths of red and orange manage to shine through, and so we often have grand and colorful displays.

The more dust there is in the atmosphere, the more colorful the sky appears. In 1883, when the Indonesian volcanic island of Krakatau exploded, it sent millions of tons of smoke, fine dust, and ash into the

We have spectacular red sunsets, and sunrises, when the air is filled with fine dust grains of ash and other aerosols. Because the Sun's rays shine through the greatest thickness of atmosphere when the Sun is close to the horizon, the shorter wavelengths of blue get absorbed. Only the longer wavelengths of red and orange manage to get through and reach our eyes.

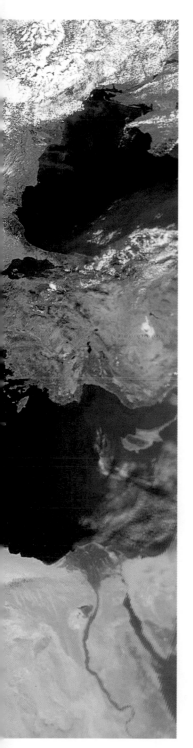

air, which the global winds then carried around the world. For about a year, people in many countries saw spectacular sunsets and sunrises that were strangely beautiful, by being tinted with green.

THE MERRY DANCERS

In 1585 thousands of terrified people ran from their homes in the French countryside to seek safety in their local churches. "The sky is on fire!" some shouted as they fled. Many thought the end of the world had come. But the next morning all was well, and the world was still there.

Perhaps the grandest display of color the atmosphere provides is the northern lights. Those who have seen a truly spectacular display say it is a sight they will never forget. The lights may appear dimly at dusk and then blend for several hours into different glowing colors and graceful, shimmering forms. At first they may color the graying sky in a great arc of yellowish or greenish white light. Then quite suddenly the arc may change into fanlike rays that blaze into pink, purple, and red. Pastel cosmic draperies might quiver and billow like a curtain blowing in a gentle breeze. The lights may fill the entire northern sky. Then gradually the forms dissolve, the intense colors fade, and the sky is left bathed in a faint glow.

On July 18, 2000, a gigantic cloud of tan dust blown off Africa's Sahara region drifted northward toward Greece and nearly covered the boot of Italy, as seen in this satellite image. Many soil-fortifying nutrients, disease germs, and other products are carried thousands of miles from one continent to another by these global dust storms.

From time to time magnetic storms on the Sun send gales of charged particles—electrons and protons—sweeping through the Solar System. When they reach Earth they are attracted by the planet's north and south magnetic poles and so enter the atmosphere most strongly at high latitudes near the poles. As the particles rain down into the upper air they collide with atoms and molecules of mostly oxygen and nitrogen.

Each time an oxygen atom is struck, it gives off a little burst of energy that we see as green, pink, or reddish light. When nitrogen atoms are struck, they give off little bursts of violet light. While light flashes from nitrogen occur about 70 miles (113 kilometers) above the ground, the oxygen flashes come from heights between 125 and 250 miles (200 to 400 kilometers). These eerily beautiful light shows are also known as the aurora borealis, the Merry Dancers, and the northern dawn.

The atmosphere clearly is a high-traffic zone. The gases, volcanic ash, cosmic dust, salt spray, and other materials that nature pours into the atmosphere all play a part in how sunlight behaves in the air. Rainbows and the northern lights are just two of the more dazzling results. But what about the other substances that are part of the air as well—the millions of tons of chemicals and gases we send skyward day and night. How do they affect the health of the atmosphere, the planet, and us?

Blobs of colorful light appear to be raining to Earth during this extraordinary display of northern lights as seen from Alaska. Notice that the stars are visible through the thin veils of reddish light. These light displays are caused by "storms" of protons and electrons streaming into Earth's atmosphere from the Sun.

FIVE

OUR
UNCLEAN SKY

People have been dumping unwanted substances into the atmosphere ever since the earliest humans discovered that they could create fire. The fumes and particles simply drifted off harmlessly and disappeared into the air. As life progressed over the thousands of years since that first fire, Earth's billions of people have produced ever bigger fires as well as machines and products that assault the atmosphere with some 50,000 chemicals that do not occur in nature. In addition, we release greenhouse gases that are changing the makeup of the atmosphere at a pace that many scientists find alarming and dangerous. Just what are all of these chemicals and greenhouse gases? What are they doing to us and the air we breathe?

Among human activities, exhaust gases from the ever-growing number of trucks and automobiles, as in this Bangkok scene, are a major source of atmospheric pollution.

A Planet-sized Greenhouse

The atmosphere contains several gases that we call *greenhouse gases*. They include methane, nitrous oxide, and carbon dioxide. By far the most important greenhouse gas is carbon dioxide, the waste gas that we exhale as we breathe. The greatest amount of carbon dioxide added to the air each day comes not from people but from factory chimneys and automobile exhaust pipes. Today more than 6.3 billion tons of carbon are poured into the atmosphere every year. An additional 1.6 billion tons are pumped into the air each year by fires set on purpose to clear land for farming.

This large volume of carbon dioxide accounts for two-thirds of the heat produced in the atmosphere. All of the greenhouse gases hang in the lower

atmosphere and act like the glass of a greenhouse. The Sun's rays easily move down through the atmosphere and warm the ground. As the ground absorbs energy from the Sun, it turns some of that energy into heat in the form of *infrared radiation*. But unlike the Sun's incoming rays, the infrared heat that rises from the land is unable to pass back up through the atmosphere. Instead, it is trapped by the greenhouse gases and so keeps our planet warm.

The process, called the *greenhouse effect*, is essential to life on Earth. However, Earth's greenhouse gases are acting much like a heavy blanket covering you on a hot summer night, keeping things *much* too warm. Most scientists are convinced that the buildup of greenhouse gases in Earth's

Top: The hothouse heat on Venus, where the air temperature is hot enough to melt lead, is caused by the high concentration of carbon dioxide in Venus's atmosphere. Probably most blue wavelengths of the Sun's light get absorbed, allowing mainly orange and red wavelengths to shine through. Such conditions would make Venus's sky red instead of blue.

Left: Shaved with a chain saw, these once luxuriant mountain slopes of Washington have been reduced to rubble and rock by the abusive practice of forest clearcutting. The former biologically rich diversity of a clearcut forest is lost, because once the loggers move on, the Forest Service replants the area with only a few tree species valued by the lumber industry.

atmosphere is overheating the planet in a process known as *global warming*. And the chief culprit is carbon dioxide.

Since the mid–1700s, human activity has increased the amount of carbon dioxide in the air by a little more than 30 percent. Since 1958 the level has increased 17 percent, and scientists estimate that by the year 2050 the carbon dioxide content in our air will have doubled. Clearly, this is an alarming trend. Venus's atmosphere is almost all carbon dioxide, and the greenhouse effect there keeps that planet's surface at a temperature of 900 degrees Fahrenheit (482 °C), hot enough to melt lead!

Climatologists, scientists who study the atmosphere, agree that the huge amounts of carbon dioxide we emit into the air are causing world temperatures to rise. In fact, there has already been a measurable rise in temperature of 1 degree Fahrenheit (0.5 °C) over the past hundred years. The trend is expected to increase, with some scientists forecasting a surface temperature rise of between 3 and 8 degrees Fahrenheit (1.5 and 4.5 °C). That may not seem like much, but it is a lot on a global scale. It took only an 8 degree Fahrenheit (4.5 °C) rise in temperature to bring the planet out of the last ice age about 18,000 years ago. At that time parts of North America were buried beneath a two-mile (3.2-kilometer) thick layer of ice.

About the only thing climatologists don't agree on is when we will really notice a significant change in our climate. Some say about the year 2050. By that time, Omaha can expect to have twenty-one days, instead of the current

These mountain peaks sticking up through Greenland's 1,000-foot (3,360-meter) thick ice cap are a reminder of what parts of North America were like at the peak of the last ice age some 18,000 years ago.

three, when summer temperatures rise above 100 degrees Fahrenheit (40 °C). New York City can expect four such days instead of none; Chicago, Illinois, six instead of none; Denver, Colorado, sixteen instead of none, Memphis, Tennessee, forty-two instead of four; and Dallas, Texas, seventy-eight instead of nineteen.

Some early warning signs of global warming may include the melting of *glaciers* in the Andes mountains and elsewhere. Sea levels would rise as a result of the increased melting of the Antarctic and Greenland *ice caps*. Since water expands when it is heated, sea level rises when the oceans heat up, and they have warmed dramatically in the last forty years. So much heat being stored in the oceans means the atmosphere is bound to heat up in the future. The climate has already begun to change, and we must be prepared for more effects of global warming to appear in the years ahead.

Weather patterns will most likely shift, and storms will be more severe. Some farming regions could be harmed while others could benefit. Many areas can expect more intense heat waves with little cooling at night. Droughts in dry regions will last longer, while other areas will experience increased flooding due to more powerful storms. As the sea level rises, long stretches of coast, such as Florida and the shores of Maryland, will be permanently flooded, forcing mass evacuations of millions of people. In spite of warnings from climatologists, governments have been slow to reduce emissions of carbon dioxide into the atmosphere, or they have done nothing at all. This is especially true of the United States.

GLOBAL WARMING AND DISEASE

As world temperatures continue to rise, billions of disease germs thriving in the increased heat pose serious health problems in several parts of the world. Disease experts think the situation is bound to get worse. The chief culprits are mosquitoes. These flying insects infect humans with diseases such as malaria, dengue fever, yellow fever, and encephalitis. A mosquito gets a malaria parasite, for instance, when it ingests the blood of a person

Lumber mills, such as this one in British Columbia, are among the many industrial sites that pollute our air, rivers, and oceans. In some paper mill towns, the air sometimes becomes so foul that it is difficult to breathe and erodes the paint finish on automobiles.

with the disease. The parasite develops inside the mosquito. When the mosquito then bites a healthy person, it passes on the parasite.

Mosquitoes breed faster and bite more as the air becomes warmer. Floodwaters create stagnant pools where the mosquitoes lay their eggs. Malaria already kills 3,000 people a day, and most of those killed are children. With global warming, malaria is now reappearing in places farther north and south of the tropics because mosquitoes are thriving in the now warmer regions. The United States, once nearly free of malaria, has seen outbreaks in Texas, Florida, Georgia, Michigan, New Jersey, and New York. The disease made its comeback during the 1990s, which was the hottest decade on record.

Dengue fever is also spreading, afflicting people with high fevers, headaches, severe joint pains, and a rash—and it can be fatal. Presently there is no known cure for the disease, and neither drugs nor vaccines to treat or prevent it. Over the past ten years, dengue fever has broadened its range, creeping from the Tropics farther into the Americas.

Can climate change alone cause the spread of disease and give rise to those wild outbreaks called epidemics? In some cases yes, in others no. For example, deforestation, not climate alone, has forced some new diseases out of the tropical rain forests. Major shifts in population and overpopulation can also cause outbreaks. So can the fact that more and more people are traveling—and carrying germs—to and from all parts of the world. Disease spreads for many reasons, and global warming is certainly helping it along.

THREE POLLUTANTS AND WHAT THEY DO

Most of the pollutants that cause health problems and global warming hang heavily in the air over large cities. They come from stoves, furnaces, factories, oil refineries, smelters, engines, and, most of all, automobile exhausts. All these things burn the fossil fuels coal, oil, gasoline, and kerosene. And because those fossil fuels are not burned very efficiently—meaning completely—they release harmful and deadly substances that cause lung diseases and ailments, including emphysema, cancer, bronchitis, and asthma. They also damage our lakes, streams, groundwater, forests, crops, and even our buildings. There are many of these harmful pollutants. Here are three.

Sulfur—When coal is burned, its sulfur combines with oxygen in the air to form the noxious (poisonous) gas, sulfur dioxide (SO_2). Huge clouds of poisonous coal smog killed 2,200 London residents in 1880, killed another 50 people in Donora, Pennsylvania, in 1948, and caused the deaths of

These fir and spruce trees in the North Carolina mountains have been killed by a combination of acid rain and insects. Acid rain and acid fog are produced when sulfur from factory chimneys combines with water vapor in the air and turns into sulfuric acid.

another 4,000 Londoners in 1952. The world's ten most heavily polluted cities—nine in China, one in India—all burn large amounts of coal. When sulfur reacts with water in the atmosphere, it produces sulfuric acid (H_2SO_4), which, mixed with water vapor, forms acid fog or falls to the ground as acid rain. Both seriously damage forests and erode metal, paint, and stone.

Nitrogen—Nitrogen combines with oxygen at high temperatures to form the poisonous gas nitrogen dioxide (NO_2). The main source of this deadly reddish brown gas is automobile engines. But it is produced in other ways as well. X-ray films once caught fire in a Cleveland, Ohio, hospital and released enough NO_2 to kill 125 people. A related gas, nitric oxide (NO), is released high in the atmosphere by jet engines. It attacks the protective *ozone layer* in the stratosphere by breaking down the ozone into NO_2 and O_2. The nitrogen dioxide then combines with an oxygen atom and produces additional nitric oxide. That means there is now more oxide available to continue to break down still more ozone.

Coal—Burning coal produces two major air pollutants—sulfur (*see above*) and particles that include soot and dust. Coal particles are inhaled deep into the lungs and just stay there, clogging them. Cities that use large amounts of coal—such as Beijing and Shanghai in China, and Calcutta in India—expose millions of adults and children to deadly mixtures of sulfur dioxide, nitrogen oxide, and coal particles every day. Worldwide, cooking with coal indoors kills some 2 million people a year, mostly women and children. Coal also may contain the poisonous substances arsenic, lead, mercury, and fluorine. In China, where 800 million people cook with coal, thousands of arsenic poisoning cases and millions of fluorine poisoning cases have been reported.

WHAT HAPPENS TO ALL THE CARBON?

There is a mystery scientists are desperate to solve: the case of the missing carbon. Of the 6 to 7 billion tons of carbon released into the atmosphere as carbon dioxide each year, we know that about 3 billion tons stay in the air while another 2 billion tons are soaked up by the oceans. But scientists can't account for the remaining 1 to 2 billion tons. Where is it hiding? If we want to know the future impact of global warming, it is important to find out. Some suspect that the missing carbon gets locked up in the boreal forests—that broad band of evergreen trees that circles Earth at high northern latitudes between 43 degrees and 65 degrees.

No matter where the missing carbon is, the fact remains that there is too much of it in the atmosphere. Some experts are wondering if there might be ways we can capture at least some of that unwanted carbon and store it where it can't do any harm. One scheme would have chemical factories, electric power plants, and natural gas drilling rigs, for example, capture the carbon dioxide they produce and inject it into the ocean or underground. One natural-gas producer drilling in the North Sea currently pumps its waste carbon dioxide 3,280 feet (1,000 meters) into the sea floor, where it will be stored for thousands of years. But it does that to avoid paying Norway's heavy carbon dioxide tax. In 1998 oil field workers pumped some 43 million tons of carbon dioxide into the ground at more than 65 oil-drilling sites. But that is only a tiny fraction when we consider all the carbon dioxide released into the air worldwide.

Despite how effective the schemes may be, one large question remains: is the idea safe and environmentally sound? To date, no one has found a reliable answer. Some say the oil and natural gas companies pumping carbon dioxide into the ground deserve praise for doing at least something to protect the environment. While this measure does help, the companies actually have quite different motives in mind. By forcing the gas into the great underground caverns of crude oil, they increase the pressure there, which makes removing the oil easier.

WHERE DO WE GO FROM HERE?

Natural forces, unaided by humans, will continue to change the global climate as they have for hundreds of millions of years. The world's population continues to grow at breakneck speed. So, more and more people have to be fed, clothed, provided with clean air, and served by a seemingly limitless number of industrial products. To provide all those necessities and luxuries means grinding up forests, pumping oil and natural gas out of the ground, damming rivers, and significantly changing the environment in many other ways. In the process, our two most precious natural resources—air and water—are being threatened with pollutants.

The famous biologist Sir Julian Huxley (1881–1975) once said that in his view the world's population should not be more than 1 billion to ensure the best quality of life for everyone. Today the world population is more than 6 billion, and in 2050 it will probably reach 9 billion. We don't yet know what effects the growing number of people will have on the environment, but one thing seems likely: we will continue to be rooted in satisfying our present needs and wants, with little thought for the future.

Competition for many things basic to our survival will probably grow intense. Clean water will be one resource that may be scarce, although we can purify water and store it for future use. But what about clean air? Will there come a time when air will have to be purified, stored under pressure in huge tanks, and piped into our homes so that we may safely breathe? Such scenarios may seem ridiculous now, but they may come true in the future.

Nothing we do can halt or reverse a major climate trend overnight. So while we are not in a position to control the atmosphere any more than we can control the climate, our collective actions become more and more important in influencing climate. Those actions might include conservation on all levels and increased climate monitoring by scientists. We have tremendous power. Whether we will use it to make the air cleaner remains to be seen.

GLOSSARY

atmospheric pressure The weight of the air pushing against you or any object. At sea level the atmospheric pressure is 14.7 pounds per square inch (6.7 kilograms per square centimeter).

climate A region's weather averaged over a long span of time. From the Greek word *klima*, meaning "slope" or "incline," and referring to the degree of slant of the Sun's rays relative to Earth's surface.

compound Any substance formed by the bonding of different kinds of atoms into molecules; for example, the joining of one atom of carbon and one atom of oxygen to form a molecule of carbon monoxide.

crustal plates The six major rock platforms and about a dozen smaller ones that form Earth's crust. The continents, along with sections of the ocean floor, are pushed about like giant rafts of stone floating in the mantle, the sea of molten rock beneath.

cyanobacteria Among the earliest bacteria that made their own food by combining water vapor and carbon dioxide from the atmosphere. Cyanobacteria have survived for more than three billion years.

doldrums The region of ocean near the Equator known for its light or calm and variable winds.

element Any substance made up of atoms that are all alike and all have the same number of protons; for example, gold, sulfur, and oxygen are elements. An element cannot be broken down into or built up from a simpler substance by chemical means.

glacier Any mass of moving land ice formed out of compacted snow.

greenhouse effect The process by which gases in the atmosphere trap heat by blocking infrared radiation emitted by Earth's surface.

greenhouse gases Gases that contribute to the greenhouse effect, including carbon dioxide, nitrous oxide, methane, and water vapor.

high-pressure system A mass of air in which the gas molecules are tightly packed and collide forcefully.

horse latitudes The high-pressure belt of air forming at about 30 degrees north and south latitudes.

ice cap An extensive ice sheet such as that covering Greenland and Antarctica.

infrared radiation Heat produced when the Sun's rays warm the ground. The wavelengths of infrared radiation are a little longer than the red wavelengths at one end of the visible spectrum and are invisible. We feel them as heat.

jet stream A high-altitude, fast-moving flow of westerly flowing air. The stream is at an altitude of 10 to 15 miles (16 to 25 kilometers) above Earth and flows along at a speed of about 250 or more miles (402 kilometers) per hour.

low-pressure system A mass of air in which the gas molecules are loosely packed and the collisions between them relatively weak.

mesosphere The layer of atmosphere immediately above the stratosphere and below the thermosphere.

molecule The smallest piece of an element or a compound that continues to have the same chemical and physical properties.

outgassing The process by which gases and other materials are released from volcanoes or other ruptures in Earth's crust and add materials to the atmosphere.

ozone layer A layer of a gas in the upper atmosphere, composed of three atoms of oxygen (O_3), which protects living organisms by filtering out a large amount of ultraviolet radiation.

phlogiston An imagined ingredient of most substances, "discovered" in the 1600s and thought both to cause burning and to be lost during burning.

planetesimals Chunks of rock, metals, and ices that were formed in the early life of the Solar System some 4.6 billion years ago, then collected and grew and eventually became the planets.

polar easterlies Belts of winds occurring at extreme latitudes in both hemispheres. They blow out of the northeast in the Northern Hemisphere and out of the southeast in the Southern Hemisphere.

prevailing westerlies Winds that travel out of the west from about 35 degrees north and south latitudes to about 55 degrees. Those in the Northern Hemisphere blow out of the southwest and those in the Southern Hemisphere out of the northwest.

silicates The largest class of minerals, containing the elements silicon and oxygen. Sand, for instance, is silicon dioxide (SiO_2).

stratosphere The layer of atmosphere lying above the troposphere and below the mesosphere.

thermosphere The top layer of Earth's atmosphere, which begins at a height of about 50 miles (80 kilometers) and blends with outer space.

trade winds The two wind belts extending from the margin of the doldrums to about 30 degrees north and south latitudes. In the Northern Hemisphere they blow out of the northeast and in the Southern Hemisphere out of the southeast.

troposphere The layer of atmosphere extending from the ground to a height of about 7 miles (12 kilometers), where most weather occurs.

ultraviolet radiation Short-wave radiation from the Sun; the harmful radiation that causes sunburn and skin cancer. Most ultraviolet radiation is absorbed by the ozone layer in the upper atmosphere.

wavelength The distance from the crest of one wave (of light, heat, or other forms of electromagnetic energy) to the crest of the next wave; a unit of measure for light.

FURTHER READING

The following books are suitable for young readers who want to learn more about the atmosphere.

Bergethon, Peter R. *The Atmosphere: An Ocean of Air, Student Science Journal*. Holliston, MA: Symmetry Learning Systems, 1999.

Fisher, Marshall. *The Ozone Layer*. New York: Chelsea House, 1992.

Hoff, Mary King, and Mary M. Rodgers. *Atmosphere*. Minneapolis, MN: Lerner Publications, 1995.

Nardo, Don. *Ozone*. San Diego, CA: Lucent Books, 1991.

Rauzon, Mark J. *The Sky's the Limit: All About the Atmosphere*. Brookfield, CT: Millbrook Press, 1999.

Walker, Jane, and Richard Rockwood. *Air*. Brookfield, CT: Millbrook Press, 1998.

WEBSITES

The following Internet sites offer information about and pictures of the atmosphere, many of them with links to other sites.

http://kids.earth.nasa.gov/air.htm   This site explains how NASA missions collect data that tell us more about the composition, behavior, and quality of our air. That information lets scientists develop and change their theories about climate and its effects. Includes links to sites that graph Earth's ozone activity and explain why air pressure is so important.

http://www.epa.gov/ebtpages.air.html   This Website was created by the Environmental Protection Agency. It includes information on all aspects of the atmosphere and how it affects us, including pollution, acid rain, and global warming.

http://www.extremescience.com/earthsciport.htm   This site goes to extremes! It is full of information on earth sciences, including the greatest earthquake, the greatest volcanic eruption, the greatest river, and the coldest place.

http://www.lib.noaa.gov/docs/education.html   This educational site provides links to more than one hundred educational sites as well as links to many other Earth, ocean, and atmosphere educational sites. It also links to organizations devoted to science education.

BIBLIOGRAPHY

These are the resources that were used in researching this book.

Allègre, Claude J., and Stephen H. Schneider. "The Evolution of the Earth," in "Revolutions in Science," a special report by *Scientific American*, 1999, pp. 4–11.

Battan, Louis J. *The Unclean Sky*. Garden City, NY: Anchor Books, 1966.

Brown, Lester R., et al. *Vital Signs: The Environmental Trends That Are Shaping Our Future*. New York: W.W. Norton for WorldWatch Institute, 2000.

Brown, Lester R., et al. *State of the World 2001*. New York: W. W. Norton for WorldWatch Institute, 2001.

Cook, J. Gordon. *Our Astonishing Atmosphere*. New York: The Dial Press, 1957.

Craig, Richard A. *The Edge of Space*. Garden City, NY: Anchor Books, 1968.

Epstein, Paul R. "Is Global Warming Harmful to Health?" *Scientific American*, August 2000, pp. 50–57.

Flanagan, Ruth. "Engineering a Cooler Planet," *Earth*, October 1996, pp. 34–39.

Flavin, Christopher, and Odil Tunali. *Climate of Hope: New Strategies for Stabilizing the World's Atmosphere*. WorldWatch Paper 130. WorldWatch Institute, June 1996.

_____. *Slowing Global Warming: A Worldwide Strategy*. WorldWatch Paper 91. WorldWatch Institute, October 1989.

Gallant, Roy A., and Christopher J. Schuberth. *Earth: The Making of a Planet*. Tarrytown, NY: Marshall Cavendish, 1998.

Gallant, Roy A. *Rainbows, Mirages, and Sundogs*. New York: Macmillan, 1987.

_____. *Earth's Changing Climate*. New York: Four Winds Press, 1979.

Goody, Richard M., and James C. G. Walker. *Atmospheres*. Englewood Cliffs, NJ: Prentice Hall, 1972.

Herzog, Howard, Baldur Eliasson, and Olav Kaarstad. "Capturing Greenhouse Gases," *Scientific American*, February 2000, pp. 72–79.

Kargel, Jeffrey S., and Robert G. Strom. "Global Climate Change on Mars," a special report by *Scientific American*, 1997.

Karl, Thomas R., and Kevin E. Trenberth. "The Human Impact on Climate," *Scientific American*, December 1999, pp. 100–105.

Loebsack, Theo. *Our Atmosphere*. New York: Pantheon Books, 1959.

Pendick, Daniel. "Fires in the Sky," *Earth*, June 1996, p. 20.

_____. "The Greatest Catastrophe," *Earth*, February 1997, p. 34.

_____. "Thunderstorm in a Box," *Earth*, December 1997, pp. 40–49.

Perkins, Sid. "Dust, the Thermostat," *Science News*, September 29, 2001, pp. 200–202.

Raloff, Janet. "Ill Winds," *Science News*, October 6, 2001, pp. 218–220.

Suplee, Curt. "Unlocking the Climate Puzzle," *National Geographic*, May 1998, pp. 38–59.

Tibbetts, John. "Plagued by Climate," *Earth*, April 1996, p. 20.

York, Derek. "The Earliest History of the Earth," *Scientific American*, January 1993, pp. 90–96.

INDEX

Page numbers in **boldface**
are illustrations.

About the Author

Roy A. Gallant, called "one of the deans of American science writers for children" by *School Library Journal*, is the author of almost one hundred books on scientific subjects, including the best-selling National Geographic Society's *Atlas of Our Universe*. Among his many other books are *When the Sun Dies*; *Earth: The Making of a Planet*; *Before the Sun Dies*; *Earth's Vanishing Forests*; *The Day the Sky Split Apart*, which won the 1997 John Burroughs award for nature writing; and *Meteorite Hunter*, a collection of accounts about his expeditions to Siberia to document major meteorite impact crater events. His most recent award is a lifetime achievement award presented to him by the Maine Library Association.

From 1979 to 2000, (professor emeritus) Gallant was director of the Southworth Planetarium at the University of Southern Maine. He has taught astronomy there and at the Maine College of Art. For several years he was on the staff of New York's American Museum of Natural History and a member of the faculty of the museum's Hayden Planetarium. His specialty is documenting on film and in writing the history of major Siberian meterorite impact sites. To date, he has organized eight expeditions to Russia and is planning his ninth, which will take him into the Altai Mountains near Mongolia. He has written articles about his expeditions for *Sky & Telescope* magazine and for the journal *Meteorite*. Professor Gallant is a fellow of the Royal Astronomical Society of London and a member of the New York Academy of Sciences. He lives in Rangeley, Maine.